A Pocketbook of Hope
In Tough Economic Times
Including
A Work at Home Job
Directory

Also by Princess Clark-Wendel, MBA

How We Can Reclaim the American Dream

A Pocketbook of Hope
In Tough Economic Times
Including
A Work at Home Job
Directory

PRINCESS CLARK-WENDEL, MBA

PRINCESS CLARK CONSULTING, INC.

A Pocketbook of Hope in Tough Economic Times Including a Work at
Home Job Directory
Copyright ©2009 by Princess Clark-Wendel, MBA
All rights reserved.

This edition published by Princess Clark Consulting, Inc.
For information, address:
Princess Clark Consulting
1220 Canterbury
Glenview, IL   60025

ISBN: 1442100206

Manufactured in the United States of America

Contents

Acknowledgements

I would like to acknowledge the Father of Telecommuting, Mr. Jack Niles for bringing the work at home industry to the forefront and creating innovative opportunities for Americans across the nation. Many thanks to all the at home workers that talked to me about their work at home experiences. A special thank you goes to the firms that provided assistance in helping me to understand their wants and needs from an employer's perspective. Without the loving support of my heavenly Father, and my family which include; Rainer, Michael, Maya, Hershelle, Arnelle and Uncle Richard, this guide would not be possible.

Disclaimer

The author of this guide book is presenting in this book her observations and personal experience of the various work at home opportunities that exist today. She is not endorsing any employer, firm or organization. Job and opportunity seekers should completely investigate all opportunities prior to making any type of commitment. This guide book is not intended to replace traditional methods of job search, but to serve as an additional source for job and opportunity seekers. This book is based on research, interviews and real life work experiences. Dates, names, locations and actual events may have been change.

Purpose

The purpose of this Pocketbook of Hope is to not only teach Americans about the work at home industry, but also to give them a running start in securing real work at home employment. In history, Americans have often been called to fight for life, liberty and justice; today many are being called to fight for the health and sustenance of their families. Working at home is one weapon to add to the arsenal. This guide provides real life tactics that can be used immediately to generate a full, part-time or supplemental income.

Introduction

In tough economic times, American's get tough. In business, this process is called innovation. Organizations innovate in order to stay competitive in an ever changing market place. Generally if organizations fail to innovate, they fail to exist or lose market share to organizations that do innovate. Consider the history of one of America's oldest retailers, K-mart that was slow to innovate at a critical time in American history and saw its market share decline to its closest competitors. In the 80's, while their competitors were investing in infrastructure and technology K-mart slept and all these years later, K-mart is still trying to recover while Wal-Mart and Target enjoy record sales year after year. Savvy innovators, innovate in both good and bad times, but sometimes, like now when many are forced to look at their finances and careers, life requires them to make tough decisions.

In talking with American's about their careers and finances, there are a few common things that they worry about in this economy. Some of the most common things are everyday short-term bread and butter issues like healthcare and meeting everyday living costs like rent, fuel and utilities, as well as their long term goals of retirement and providing a college education for their children. Of course, when short term bread and butter issues are becoming more and more difficult to meet, sadly, long term goals, like retirement, going back to college, and the dream of purchasing a second home, are often swept under the carpet and never realized. Because so many Americans are constantly worrying about these things, their interpersonal relationships are also suffering which causes another downhill spiral. Indeed, these are tough times.

Although terms like innovation and change are business concepts, *A Pocketbook of Hope* is not about the macro implications of innovation and change. Surely, there is not much that individuals can do change the macro, unless they begin to deal with the micro issues that are affecting them. Inefficient government, poor oversight and unsettling financial markets will not change overnight, but individually, everyone can change if they have will and means to do it. This guide is about how to apply business concepts to help make innovative choices about how to earn a living in a tough economy. One way to resolve some of the challenges plaguing the American middle class is through work at home options. Unfortunately, these options may not work for everyone, but for those who do find it helpful, they may enjoy a greater sustainability than their out of work counterparts using traditional methods to earn an income.

CHAPTER ONE

ABOUT THE WORK AT HOME

INDUSTRY

"An employee working at home one or two days per week can save a corporation $6000 – $12,000 per year."

--Jack Niles, The Founder of Telecommuting

The work at home industry was born from the early ambitions of its founder, Jack Niles. Jack Niles, a Physicist is considered the Father of Telecommuting. Since 1973, he has worked with leaders and organizations to change the way in which people work. His hands on research have also led him to develop several studies and books on telecommuting.

It is noted that telecommuting has been around for a long

time, but only until recently has it become more main stream. As technology and global partnerships have grown and emerged so has the acceptability and need for telecommuting and work at home alternatives. A nation's desire to live cleaner and greener lives has also fueled the rise of the industry. In 1996, the United States Congress adopted the Clean Air Act amendments in hopes of reducing carbon dioxide and ground-level ozone levels (Siano, 1998). This amendment was especially important because it prompted large organizations, including the government to encourage alternative work methods that eventually led to more and more people taking part in job sharing and telecommuting.

Over the years, telecommuting has played a drastic part in transforming the environment, especially in large urban areas. In cities like Chicago, LA, and New York which are known very positively for their industry and enterprise but is considered infamous for fueling high levels of congestion and pollution caused primarily by the large amounts of traffic. The explosion in urban populations does more than just impact traffic, congestion and pollution it also increases America's dependence on foreign oil. Understandably, this is problematic because as more and more oil is consumed, the more individuals eventually pay at the pump and in heating their homes, resulting in less money in their pocketbooks and wallets to pay for everyday living expenses and long term goals. Thus, many Americans feel, and some are indeed poorer because of the nations dependence on foreign oil, working at home helps to decrease this dependency.

It is widespread knowledge that many of America's roads and bridges are in dire straits. Therefore, any reduction of pollution and use of American highways would prove helpful to the economy and infrastructure. Although change is coming in regards to restoring many of the nation's bridges and infrastructure, which again, is on the macro level and will hopefully, occur over time. On the micro level, individual Americans have been helpful in alleviating traffic congestion, and stress from navigating the busy highways by working at home.

CHAPTER TWO

WHAT WORKING AT HOME LOOKS LIKE TODAY

The first telecommuter on record was a Boston bank president, who arranged to have a phone line strung from his office to his home in Somerville, Massachusetts, in 1877. No one called it telecommuting then. It was just smart business
                    --June Langhoff, The
                    Telecommuter's Advisor

Today, more than in any other era in history, American's need new

and innovative ways to earn an income. One of the foremost

reasons lies in the state of the American economy and the

uncertainty that is plaguing the nation from small town America to

uptown American. Signs of this downfall began with the rising costs

of oil and then spiraled out of control when the housing crisis

erupted. These two shocks affected not only Wall Street, but Main

Street where many Americans live.

American's earning less, but working more is not a not a new thing. The buying power of the dollar has been slumping considerably over the years.   Sadly, many American's have grown accustomed to supplementing their income to pay for many things that used to be purchased with a single wage owner and job, like a nice vacation, college credit or savings for retirement. It has turned into far more than simply fulfilling a want or long-term goal but instead has become a necessity for survival. Without options, the freedom and independence that many Americans once enjoyed is being put in jeopardy. Daily, Americans are shown footage from the media of more and more of their counterparts being added to unemployment rolls, requiring government assistance for housing and food. This should not be the picture that is portrayed to future generations, as Generation X and Y are considered the most innovative generations of our time and has changed the way the world communicates. The same spirit of innovation that has spurred new technology must also possess the spirit of individual Americans to change the way they think about think about providing for their

families.

CHAPTER THREE

An Employer's Perspective

"If you don't include telecommuting in your program, your company will not be competitive."
--Garry Mathiason, Partner,
Littler, Mendelson, Fastiff,
Tichy & Mathiason Law Firm

Work at home options is not only ripe for individuals, but organizations as well. As government, consumers and shareholders call for organizational accountability and fair business practices, employers are being forced to do more with less. Some of these methods include reductions in salaries and bonuses. Needless to say, but, they too are looking for innovative business practices and tools to fight the economic downturn. Work at home options is one antidote that employers are using to cure their ailing bottom lines.

Consider this, many of the things that originally forced talent out of the work force like child care expenses, disability, and rising gas prices are some of the things that also make work at home options attractive to employers. For example a working mom with child care expenses exceeding $150 to $200 per week, in addition to rising gas prices generally finds herself at a crossroads as to whether or not going to work is really worth it. A woman of child bearing age can have her cake and eat it too if she can work from home because working at home lifts some of the burdens weighing on working mothers. Immediately the ills of paying for child care and gas have dissipated if a mom can work from home. Not only is this good for the her, it is also great for her employer because she can offer her employer the skills that he desperately needs at a lower "work at home rate" while still maintaining her household and employment. The organization benefits because it does not lose the talent and the employee does not lose the income. It is a win-win situation for all stakeholders. Organizations are also able to operate at a lower rate because they need less office space and sometimes instead of hiring staff as employees they are hired as independent contractors reducing many of the mandatory employer-employee burdens like workers compensation and payroll taxes.

Another noted benefit of these kinds of relationships is lower absenteeism, which can lead to improved quality and services. One large employer allows his employees to work at home 12 days out of the month and they are able to choose which days, therefore, employees are less likely to call in "sick" to take care of other things and opting instead to use their work at home day to navigate both their professional and personal lives. Generally, a happy employee provides better service which in turn, benefits the end consumer in the long run. As organizations find ways to reduce costs and improve profit, more and more of Middle America will find themselves not toiling away in corporate office, but providing core services to organizations in the comfort and confines of their home offices.

Leaders within organizations understand that as America becomes greener, they must also adapt green practices. As mentioned earlier, work- at- home arrangements reduce traffic congestion especially in large urban areas and it also improves the environment in other ways. Working at home encourages the use of more technology which reduces paperwork thus, playing a little part in saving trees and some would even argue consumption is even reduced. Consider this; does one drink more coffee at the office or at home?

As firms participate in green initiatives, their public relations, marketing and recruiting is also improved. Who doesn't want to work for a green firm, which is also family friendly and allows their employees to work from home? Gen X and Y are fiercely passionate about the environment; therefore any organization that is in line with their concerns not only has their attention, but also their skills, and services as employees or independent contractors and money as consumers of their wares and services. In a competitive and complex marketplace, organizations that are sensitive to the needs of people and the environment will fare better than their unsympathetic counterparts.

CHAPTER FOUR

WHERE THE INDUSTRY IS HEADED

Telecommuters outperform their peers at the traditional office by 16 percent.
>   *--The Training Magazine,*
>   *1994*

Surely, the industry is on the rise. As employers continue to downsize, by reducing their workforce and merging jobs, more American's are beginning to feel the pressure to innovate and think differently about how they earn money. Of course, this will cause a lot of pain on Main Street, but in most cases, pain leads to change and causes most to rethink their strategies and retool. Hopefully, this retooling will prompt many American's to view their wealth of collateral consisting of their talent, skills and abilities as business tools, which will lead them to make business decisions that will not only provide them with meaningful employment, but also unlimited opportunity, success and stability. The work at home industry is an opportunity for those seeking to jump on the bandwagon now, while it's hot. There is an old saying about striking an iron while it's hot, not only is working at home hot, it's sexy.

Those contemplating entering the work at home industry should not enter it as a jilted lover scorned by his or her last organization. They should approach the opportunity to provide services to an employer while working at home as a first date, presenting their best faces and most polished game. As organizations, both large and small, fight for their share of an international market, amidst a startling financial backdrop crippled with tight lending and reminiscent of a ride at Six Flags, many will enter into work at home arrangements, but will do so carefully. So as in dating, if the end goal is marriage or a long-term contract then the pursuer (employee or independent contract) must continually nurture the relationship and provide reasons why the pursued (employer) can not live without the services provided by the employee or independent contractor. These reasons are things like superior service, a brilliant work product, excellent worth ethic, agreeable personality, timeliness, steadfastness and

a fair rate. If an employer can count on someone in a downtime, they will

remember them in an uptime.

CHAPTER FIVE

RELATIONSHIPS

"Never trust people's assertions, I always judge of them by their actions."
--Ann Radcliffe, The Mysteries of Udolpho, 1764

Works at home relationships vary. The most common relationship is one

most people understand and that is of an employer-employee relationship.

It is generally what is called an at-will contract which means employees are

free to quit and employers are free to fire whenever either party deem it

necessary. The employer hires the employee to perform a job like

accounting or bricklaying and the employee completes it. The only

difference is that the employee works or performs their duties primarily

from home or outside of the office. In these relationships sometimes the

employee works from home exclusively or sometimes two or three days

are spent at the office. The employer pays all the mandatory taxes and benefits and may also offer additional benefits like health care, vacation, and bonus. The employer basically controls the employee's hours and directs how the employee performs his job. If the employee requires additional training or development, usually the employer provides the training at his expense, as well as tools or equipment that is needed in order for the employee to perform his job like a laptop, hammer, etc.

Another common relationship in the work at home industry is that of an independent contractor. An independent contractor is often known by many names in the industry like Guru, service provider, freelancer, or simply contractor. They are hired by organizations to provide specific services and generally perform their duties based on a negotiated contract. They are responsible for paying their own expenses, as well as any required taxes. They also have to pay for their own health and liability insurance. In most cases, they are free to work for whom they choose and whenever they chose to work because they set their own hours. Many independent contractors have more than one contract, although some may work exclusively for one employer. In general, an independent contractor status provides more flexibility and freedom than an employer-employee relationship.

Without a doubt, the work at home employer-employee and independent contractor relationships are unique and demand a level of trust that is not seen in typical work arrangements. As in most long term relationships trust is solidified with a contract and generally that contract spells out the requirements of all the parties involved. All work at home arrangements should have a contract, but in order to deepen the relationship and secure additional work, trust must be matched with superior quality, service and attention from all parties.

CHAPTER SIX

JOBS AVAILABLE

"Life grants nothing to us mortals without hard work."

--Horace, (65 BC – 8 BC), Satires

Almost every type of position one could wish upon a star for exists

in the work at home industry, even some nurses and teachers work

from home. This is due primarily to the technological advantages of

the last two decades which have allowed people to work virtually

from anywhere. An array of people are working at home from

uptown to downtown, Main Street and to as close as your street.

Yes, many would be surprised by how many of their neighbors are

earning a meaningful income from the comfort of their homes. In

2000, more than 4.2 million of our neighbors worked from home.

Additionally, the 2000 US Census reported that Americans working

at home grew

almost 23 percent from 1990 to 2000 (US Census, 2000). In 2001, another time in American history when financial markets took a dive, the International Telework Associated reported that 28 million American were working from home (Telework, 2001).

People who work at home are more than the typical at home workers like real estate agents, farmers, and home day care operators. They are as diverse as the industries they represent. At home workers careers range from medical coders, virtual secretaries to engineers, marketing specialists, accountants and stockbrokers. Surprisingly, some manufacturing, assembly and even teaching jobs are even performed at home. Almost every industry and profession has found its face somewhere in the body of the work at home industry, sometimes on a part or full time basis. Some of the fastest growing jobs in the work at home industry include customer service, data entry, public relations, marketing, sales, administrative and IT positions.

CHAPTER SEVEN

COMPENSATION

"Too many of us look upon Americans as dollar chasers. This is a cruel libel, even if it is reiterated thoughtlessly by the Americans themselves."
--Albert Einstein

The wages of an at home worker is generally no different from the typical brick and mortar wage earner. One could even argue that the compensation of at an at home wage earner is far greater when the savings benefit is added to the scenario. Following are some of the typical wages earned by some at home worker full time wage earners from a 2007 Work At Home Study from PCC Consulting. The figure displays some of the wages typically earned by at workers. It is noted that performance based jobs like insurance and sales, generally earn a higher income; whereas task based positions like data entry clerk and administrative positions earn standard salaries. Some performance based positions even include bonuses and incentives, as well as the standard commissions.

JOB/PROFESSION	ANNUAL WAGE
Administrative Assistant (Secretary, Virtual Assistant, Office Assistant)	$25,000 to $42,000
Data Entry Clerk	$16,000 to $38,000
Paralegal	$26,500 to $51,000
Advertising Sales	$30,000 to $144,000
Accountant/Bookkeeper	$25,500 to $82,300
Insurance Agent	$16,500 to $128,000
Desktop Publisher	$27,900 to $48,000
Writer/Editor/Publisher Content Publisher	$18,000 to $62,900

At home workers can be paid either daily, weekly, bimonthly, or monthly. They are compensated based upon the contract they signed. Some work at home earners are paid at project completion. For example, an employer may contract or hire an at home content provider to write content on their website, once the content provider has completed adding the requested content to the site, he would then invoice his employer. Proper invoicing (billing) and documentation is the second most important step in ensuring accurate and timely compensation payouts. The invoice should detail the work performed, time, and bill rate. Some invoices may be based upon a contract like work completed, if so the invoice should state the work completed and the pre-negotiated rate charged on the invoice. Any additional work performed should also be listed on the invoice. For example, if the at home worker was initially contracted to answer calls from 8 am to 4 pm, but then the employer asked the contractor to provide services such as typing or mailing, the invoice must reflect the additional services and the time spent performing those services. It is best to add any changes to the initial contract in writing, especially when the employer-contractor relationship is new.

Home workers have many different ways to receive payments from the employer. One of the most popular ways is through direct deposit. Direct deposit requires the at home worker to have a checking and/or savings account, and use it to receive direct deposits or payments from their employer. Direct deposit forms can usually be obtained from the local bank, filled out with the at home workers checking or savings accounting number, routing number and home address and then given to the employer to input into his reimbursement or payables system. Other ways which are growing popular is from the use of ecommerce payment processing services. Some of the most popular ones are PayPal and Google Checkout. Even personal financial software like Quicken allows individuals to send invoices and receive payments to their bank accounts. Lastly, the traditional method of snail mail is still used even today.

In some at home work relationships, the issue of taxes is simple. If the at home worker is hired as an employee of the employer then the taxes are the responsibility of the employer. The employer withholds mandatory taxes like Social Security and Medicare, as well as unemployment insurance from their employee's compensation. One should only worry about taxes if he or she is considered an independent contractor.

CHAPTER EIGHT

TO BE OR NOT TO BE AN INDEPENDENT CONTRACTOR

"Self-reliance is the only road to true freedom, and being one's own person is its ultimate reward."
--Patricia Sampson

Today with so many opportunities to provide services while working from home, one might wonder is it better to simply work for an employer or to contract with one. An independent contractor is a business owner, who is responsible for all the things of a typical brick and mortar business owners except the at home independent contractor works from home. Some of these responsibilities include things like marketing, advertising, and taxes.

In order to be seen as a legitimate independent contractor by potential employers or clients, the independent contractor should establish credentials. Some of the credentials needed include a registered business name, business cards, and a tax ID number. If a business does not use legal name of its owner then the name must be registered in most states as an assumed name. An independent contractor can register his business name, usually at the local county clerk's office; generally a nominal fee is required to register a business name. The county clerk is also a good resource to find out if a business requires an operating permit, or business or professional license. An assumed name is needed to open a business account, otherwise independent contractors must use their individual accounts to perform business transactions. This, of course, does not make good business sense. It is never a good idea to mix business income with personal income.

The IRS has established measures to ascertain whether or not an independent contractor is acting an employee or not. This is important because some firms have been known to classify their actual "employees" as "independent contractors" in order to escape mandatory tax burdens and benefits. The IRS looks at how the independent contractor is paid, how and where he performs the work, when he performs the work and whether or not he could earn a profit or suffer a loss from engaging in the work in which he was contracted.

Another important aspect of working as an independent contractor is taxes. An independent contractor is responsible for paying his own taxes. They should save enough money from their earnings to pay their mandatory taxes each year. An easy way to do this is to pay estimated taxes on a quarterly basis. An independent contractor earning more than $3000 in business activities should consult with an accountant to get help in paying their taxes.

Like a student without his books, an independent contractor is lost without his contract or written agreement. A contract spells out the terms and conditions of both the employer and independent contractor. It will include the work and services to be performed, which is usually called the statement of work, how the employer and contractor will communication with one another, along with the payment terms and conditions. Payment terms can be at the completion of the work, weekly, bi-weekly and monthly.   A

statement of confidentiality should also be included to protect the

interests of the parties.

CHAPTER NINE

In What Ways Do People Work From Home?

"Those who would give up essential liberty to purchase a little temporary safety deserve neither liberty nor safety."
--Benjamin Franklin

Typically there are two ways to work from home, one way which was previously described is an independent contractor and the other way is as an employee. To determine which way is best, one should think about their current job and duties. For example, jobs that are primarily performed at a desk are typically ideal to work from home. These jobs include things like data entry, accounting and word processing. Although these jobs are ideal, other jobs can be performed at home as well. Jobs that involve some face time, but also some desk time can be worked from home. For example, auditing and consulting jobs can be worked at home some days of the week and other days those jobs can be performed off site at client or employer's facility. Any position that allows one to limit .human contact to some degree more than likely can be performed at home.

For earners in traditional employer-employee brick and mortar workplaces, gaining buy in from a boss to work at home may seem like a daunting task, but with a clearly defined and executed plan it can be accomplished. One way to do this is to develop a telework plan. A telework plan is a proposal that outlines positive arguments for working at home. It should include all of the benefits to both the company and employee. Some of the benefits include many of the cost reduction strategies outlined earlier like improved productivity, free up office, and the opportunity to be more creative by working independently. The plan must address checks and balances like communication and reporting issues. Savvy plan developers should research their job description and determine how others in that position are also working from home, then present those result to the employer in the plan as well. If working at home is new to the firm, then one should suggest a 60 or 90 day exploratory trial period or a plan that includes three days in the office and two at home. Like most things, a clear and developed plan will go along way in convincing an employer to consider the work at home option as a solution to reduce cost and improve productivity.

CHAPTER TEN

TOOLS & TECHNOLOGY NEEDED TO WORK FROM HOME

"This is why I loved technology, if you used it right, it could give you power and privacy."
> *--Cory Doctorow, Little Brother, 2008*

Many of the tools to maintain a successful home office are basically the same things that are seen in a traditional office without the people of course. A computer or laptop is mandatory, as well as a dedicate landline phone and fax with free long distance. Most people that work from home use headsets, this allows them to talk while typing and gives them the freedom to walk around. There is technology that can allow home workers to access other computers and this is helpful if one needs to access their computer from their brick and mortar location. One company successful in implementing this technology is GoToMyPc.com. High speed internet like DSL, Broadband or Cable is required in most cases. Today, many work at home independent contractors opt for small business service from their IT providers. This provides them with a faster internet connection and if their lines are down or there is a problem guarantees premium service. A virus protection and firewall is especially important since much of the work is access via the World Wide Web. A file cabinet is needed to store contracts and work products. Finally, the at home office should be free of noise and appear as professional as any traditional brick and mortar office.

New technology is emerging almost daily to make the work at home or virtual offices more efficient. Web conference and telepresence solutions are video meetings that allow participants to perform meetings and brainstorming sessions as if they were in a face to face meeting. Online document storage and sharing has made communication easier, and it seems the fax is slowly heading down the path of the dinosaur. Technological advancements have made working at home more convenient and efficient, especially in

today's "got to have it now" marketplace.

CHAPTER ELEVEN

THE TRUTH & NOTHING BUT THE TRUTH

"Truth is the only safe ground to stand on."
--Elizabeth Cady Stanton

It would be remiss to only discuss the upside of working at home, without elaborating on the downside. Working at home is not for everyone, although many have come to enjoy it. Someone who works from home must be able to work independently, thus working from home can be lonely. For example, one should consider how long they can go without human contact and banter before they jump into a work at home arrangement. The quiet loneliness that a work at home environment entails can be catastrophic for someone requiring human contact and entertainment which may lead to non revenue generating and costly behavior like foregoing work for sleep or human contact. As more and more employers come to understand the loneliness experienced by at home workers, some have developed social-work networks and virtual communication tools to provide feedback and support. Another aspect that is often seen as a challenge to at home workers is organization. An at home worker must have good organization and time management skills, without it one could find himself without enough time to accomplish required tasks. Inefficient time management and organization often impacts bookkeeping and payment processing. Happy at home workers have developed strategies to work productivity ensuring a successful work-life balance.

A downside even exists for employers. Although many employers enjoy greater productivity from their at home employees, some often feel the pinch in their pocketbooks, as they experience high technology costs and improvements in order to maintain their at home worker. Because of the latest technological innovations in communication, organization, time management and bookkeeping, there is currently not enough information to ascertain whether or not working in a traditional brick and mortar office is more cost effective, productive and enjoyable than working from home. Perhaps over time the economic benefit will be elucidated. To this point, however, experience with the struggles associated with a weak environment and unstable economy leading to employment uncertainty almost everywhere, further shows that working at home is one hopeful and innovative option to many navigating their lives in tough economic times.

A P P E N D I X

Recommended Sites for At Home Workers

www.workspace.liveops.com A social networking site for home workers.

- www.1099.com Magazine for independent contractors.
- www.irs.gov Resources for the small business owner.
- www.score.org Free business consulting for small business owners and independent contractors.

References

Niles, J. (1998). *Managing Telework: Strategies for Managing the Virtual Workforce.* New York. NY: John Wiley & Sons.

Siano, M. *Merging Home and Office. Telecommuting is a High-Tech Energy Saver.*

AllBusiness.com

Better Business Bureau. www.bbb.org

Emagazine.com

Entrepreneur. www.entrepreneur.com

Freelancers Union. www.freelancersunion.org

Google Cart www.google.com

Paypal for Payment Processing www.paypal.com

Small Business Administration. www.sba.gov

Tele Work Exchange. www.teleworkexchange.com

United States Census. www.census.gov

The Work at Home Job

Directory

Filled with

Virtual Employers

Job Directory

Listed in Order of Opportunity

Accounting & Management Consulting Opportunities

Actuary.com
www.actuary.com
Actuary jobs and information

Balance Your Books
www.balanceyourbooks.com
Accounting & Bookkeeping positions

Bateman & Co., Inc
www.batemanhouston.com
Accountants, Bookkeepers and interns
*Follow employment link

Bookminders
www.bookminders.com
Accounting & Sales Positions
*Follow employment link

Click Accounts
www.clickaccounts.com
Accounting, Bookkeeping & Taxes

Click N Work
www.clicknwork.com
Analysts & Consultants
*Follow opportunities link
Pay between $40 - $150 per hour
Also will consider fixed fee and commission share

CPA Moms
www.cpamoms.us
Accounting, bookkeeping, tax preparation, payroll, QuickBooks experts

DCSFI
http://www.dcfsi.com/careers.htm
Accounting, bookkeeping, tax preparation

Nationwide Loan Processing

http://www.loanprocessor.org/work-at-home-job-opportunities.html
Mortgage Processors
Pay: $3500 - $7500 month

Statewide Computerize Tax Service, Inc.
http://www.1040.com/statewidetax/

Tad Accounting
http://www.tadaccounting.com/careers.html
Accountants, Bookkeepers, CPA's

Taxhelp911
http://www.taxhelp911.com/joinus.html
Accountants & Tax Preparation

VF AuditMall
http://www.vfauditmall.com/pages/profile.asp#

VT Audit
http://www.vtaudit.com/careers.asp
Auditors, Payroll Processors, Insurance

Warrener Stewart
http://www.warrenerstewart.com/recruit.html
Accountants

Administrative Opportunities

Alderson Reporting
http://aldersonreporting.com/AldersonCareers/
Court Reporters, Stenographers, Typists

American Airlines
http://www.aacareers.com/us/frame_index.htm?http&&&www.aacareers.com/us/index.shtml
Reservation agents residing in Fort Worth, TX and Tucson Arizona

Axion Data
http://www.axiondata.com/employreq.htm
Data Entry

Caption Colorado
http://www.captioncolorado.com/application/application.htm
Full and Part time Captioning
Pay is Competitive with benefits for full time

Continental Promotion Group
http://www.cpginc.com/employment/us/homeworkerinfo.asp#dataentry
Data Entry

Dion Data
http://www.diondatasolutions.net/opportunities.htm
Data Entry, Data Management

Expedict
http://www.expedict.co.uk/work.php
Typist

Keys for Cash
https://www.keyforcash.com/
Typists

Mountain West Processing
http://www.mountainwestprocessing.com/page5.html
Transcription

Mulberry Studio
http://www.mulberrystudio.com/jobs.htm
Transcription and Proofreaders

NetTranscripts
http://www.nettranscripts.com/employment.htm
Transcription

OnSite
http://www.onss.com/careers/
Various administrative

Palm Coast Data
http://home.palmcoastd.com/pcd/pcdwebsite/pcd_careers_jobs_home.htm
l
Data Entry (Palm Coast, FL residents only)

Reed Technology
http://reedtech.com/r_postings.asp
Data Entry (Horsham, PA or Falls Church, VA residents only)

SpeakWrite
http://www.speak-write.com/TypistNav/Employment/index.cfm
Typists
Pay: $10 - $12 per hour

Team Double-Click
http://www.teamdoubleclick.com/Current_Openings.html
Administrative and Typing Positions

TigerFish
http://www.tigerfish.com/employment.html
Transcribers

Vitac
http://www.vitac.com/careers.htm
Captioners

Assembly Opportunities

American Consolidated Exchange
http://ace.allcustomexotics.com/
Assembly

Cottage Industries
www.cotind.com

Disciple's Cross
http://www.disciplescross.com/
Assembly

Elk Creek Case Company
www.besthomejobs.com
Sewing

The Ideal Craft Company Inc.
www.idealcraft.com
Assembly

Magical Gift Company
www.magicalgift.com
Sewing, Glue Gun & Paint
Phone: 860.482.3955

Tiny Details
www.tinydetails.com
Assembly

Collection

WebTracer
http://www.webtracer.com/
Skip Tracer

Customer Service

1-800 Flowers
http://ww4.1800flowers.com/template.do?id=template8&page=9000#18

Accolade Support
www.accoladesupport.com/openings.html

ACD Direct
www.ACDdirect.com

Admission Consultants
www.admissionsconsultants.com

Alpine Access
www.alpineacess.com

American Airlines
www.aa.com

Aquaricon
www.aquaricon.com

Arise
www.arise.com

ARO
www.callcenteroptions.com

ASI
www.employmentfromhome.net

Baby to Bee
www.babytobee.com

Beyond Marketing Online
www.Beyondmarketingonline.com

BRG Research Services
www.brgathome.com/applyhome1.php

CCI
www.ccicompany.us/career1.aspx

Citrix
www.citrix.com

Cloud 10
www.cloud10.com

Connect2Agent
www.Connect2Agent.com

Convergys
http://www.convergysworkathome.com/

Customer Loyalty Concepts
www.customloyal.com
Pay: $8.00 to $12.00 per hour

Customer Service Review
http://www.csr-net.com/jointeam.htm

DeRosa Communications
http://www.derosa.com/callteam.htm
Technology, financial services, medical sales, advertising and others

Expert Business Development
http://www.expertbizdev.com/join_our_team.htm
Candidate's must have a minimum of 15 years of solid business experience, preferably in sales, management or ownership.

eCallogy
www.ecallogy.com
(Utah residents only)

ESM
www.education-sales.net
(Colorado residents only)

Extended Presence
http://www.extendedpresence.com/salesjobs/JobDescription.asp?JID=51
Lead Generation & Appointment Setters
Pay $18.00 to $25.00 per hour

Fonemed
www.fonemed.com
Registered Nurses Only

GE Call Centers
www.gecallcentercareers.com
Customer Service

Grindstone
http://www.grindstone.com/career.html
Outbound Telemarketers

Green TeleServices
www.gteleservices.com

HirePoint Tel Tech
http://www.hirepoint.com/athome/index.html
Customer Service

Home Shopping Network
http://www.hsn.com/careers_at-988_xa.aspx?nolnav=1

ICT Group
http://www.ictgroup.com/index.php/careers/
Customer Management

InfoCision
http://www.infocision.com/Careers/Pages/WorkFromHome.aspx
Residents of Ohio and West Virginia
Customer Service
Pay $8.50 per hour

Intuit
https://www.quickbase.com/db/bb9zr8jnb?a=nwr

Intrep
http://www.aaarenewals.com/i_careers_RS.htm
Renewal Specialist
Pay $12.00 per hour plus bonus

J. Lodge
http://www.jlodge.com/
Call Analyst
Hires residents of Arizona, Ohio, Wisconsin, Massachusetts, Pennsylvania, Florida, Texas, North Carolina and Virginia

JetBlue Airways
http://www.jetblue.com/about/work/

Kowal & Associates
www.kowalinc.com
Send resumes: humanres@kowalinc.com .
Benefit packages

LiveOps
www.liveops.com
Various pay scale

Lunar Pages
http://www.lunarpages.com/jobs/
Various positions including Technology

Medco
www.Medcohealth.com
Select Careers

MicahTek
http://www.micahtek.com/jobs.html
Customer Service
National Telecommuting Institute, Inc.
www.nticentral.org
Hire primarily people with disabilities

N.E.W
http://www.newhomebasedccr.com/ccrfaqs.asp
Customer Service
Pay $9.00 per hour at least/On Site training for 3 to 5 weeks

Next Level Solutions
http://www.dial-nls.com/content.php?link=Careers_ind
Outbound Telemarketing
Pay $7.50 per hour plus
Send resume to Amanda Blalock ablalock@dial-nls.com

Niteo Services, Inc.
www.niteoservices.com
Click careers
Customer Support

O'Currance Teleservices
http://www.ocurrance.com/employment.php
Sales
Pay $9.00 per hour plus commission

On Point Advocacy
www.onpointathome.com
$12.00 per hour

Prince Market Research
http://pmresearch.com/employment
Telephone Interviewers
Hires in Florida, Tennessee and Texas

Progressive Business Publications
http://www.pbp.com/employment.asp
Editorial, Marketing and Audio Conference

Public Opinion Research
www.publicopinionresearch.net
Telephone Interviewers
Pay $13.25 to $25.00 per hour

SCI Live
http://www.scilive.com/call-center-careers.htm
Pay .20 per min talk time

Secure Call Management
www.sciathome.com

Service 800
www.service800.com
Customer Service

Sterling Testing Systems
www.sterlingtesting.com
Accepting applications from the following states;
California, Florida, Minnesota, Texas and Wisconsin

Support Freaks
http://www.supportfreaks.com/joinourteam.html

TeLCare
http://www.telcarecorp.com/SurveyAgent.htm
Telephone Survey Agent
Pay $9.00 to $10.00 per hour

TeleLink Call Center
http://www.telelinkcallcentre.com/contactUs/careers.asp
Canadian Residents Only

Thor Travel Services
www.thor24.com
Click agency

Time Communications
www.timecommunication.com
Minneapolis, MN residents only
W4 employee with benefits after 90 days

U-Haul
http://jobs.uhaul.com/job_detail.aspx?aval_job_id=23698&%20mode=
Customer Service

Ver-A-Fast Corporation
www.verafast.com

VIP Desk
www.vipdesk.com
VirtuServe
http://www.ccemployment.com/
Customer Service, Telemarketer, Appointment Scheduler

VoiceLog
www.voicelog.com
Pay $9.50 per call

West At Home
www.workathomeagents.com
Employee (guaranteed wage)

Westat
http://www.westat.com/atHome/index.cfm
At Home Data Collectors
Pay $8.25 per hour (English), $10.25 (Bilingual) plus $2.00 per hour additional
on weekends

Willow
www.willowcsn.com

Working Solutions
www.workingsol.com
Reservation Enrollments, Customer Services, Sales, Market Research,
Technical Support
Pay $7.00 - $30.00 per hour

XAct Telesolutions
www.Xactservices.com
Customer Service

Consultants & Professionals

About.com Guides
http://beaguide.about.com/topics.htm
Pay: at least $750 per month. Some guides earn $100k annually

Amazon.com Mechanical Turks
https://www.mturk.com/mturk/welcome
Answer Bag
www.answerbag.com
Answer questions

Brain Mass
http://www.brainmass.com/
Online Teaching Assistant for graduate students

Clarity Consultants
http://www.clarityconsultants.com/applicants.asp
Corporate management consultant jobs and project management jobs in all
sectors including education, finance, business, and software
Longer Term assignments include benefits

ContractXchange
http://www.contractxchange.com/
Various opportunities with major companies

Elance
www.elance.com

Gerson Lehrman Group Councils
https://www.glgcouncils.com/apply.aspx
Industry-focused networks of executives, physicians, scientists, engineers,
attorneys, market researchers and other professionals from around the

world. Members of the GLG Councils are compensated for consulting with global business and investment leaders on topics within their area of expertise.

Guideline
http://www.guideline.com/corporate/careers.html

HireMinds
http://www.hireminds.com/

Just Answer
http://www.justanswer.com/expert.aspx

Know Brainers
http://www.knowbrainers.com/experts.php?
Get Paid by Answering Questions from your blog

Learner's Paradise
http://www.learnersparadise.com/home/cgi-bin/homePage.pl
Online Teaching for Guru's

Live Person
https://www.liveperson.com/registration/expert-registration/expert-signup.aspx

Momentum Network
http://www.momentumnetwork.com/page.php?pg=careerop
Online Support Technicians
Graphic Designers
Database Integration Programmers
Web/Software Developers
Marketing Project Managers
Train the Trainer/Coach Specialists
Business Development Managers

National Seminars Group
http://www.nationalseminarstraining.com/CareerOpps/CareerOpps.html
Trainers

Remote Work Management
http://www.remote-work.com/fx.remotework/scheme/register.aspx

ReviewNet Services
http://www.reviewnet.net/testadvisor.htm
Technical Positions

Thesis and Dissertation Advisors
http://www.dissertationadvisors.com/
Thesis and Dissertation Consultants

Turner Consulting Group
http://www.tcg.com//index.php?option=com_content&task=view&id=56&Itemid=41
Technical

Crafting

Cash Crafters
www.cashcrafters.com

Etsy
www.etsy.com

Scrapbook
www.scrapbook.com

Data Entry

Amazon
www.mturk.com
Technical

Axion Data Services
www.axiondata.com

Continential Promotional Group
www.cpginc.com
Scottsdale Arizona

CyberSecretaries
www.typist.youdictate.com

Giving Answers LLC
www.givinganswers.com

Keys for Cash
https://www.keyforcash.com/
Typists

Keyers Online
www.keyersonline.com

Reed Technology
http://reedtech.com/r_postings.asp
Data Entry (Horsham, PA or Falls Church, VA residents only)

Education, Teaching, Tutoring & Development Opportunities

A-1 Tutor
http://a1tutor.com/
Tutors

Academic Word
http://www.academicword.com/emp.asp
Editors and Translators

Admissions Consultants
http://www.admissionsconsultants.com/employment.asp
Admission Counselors

Aim For A
http://www.aim4a.com/tutors.php
American InterContinental University Online
http://careers.aiuonline.edu/careers/
Teachers

Berlitz Language
http://careerservices.berlitz.com/current_job_vacancies.asp
Language Teachers

Bilingual America, Inc
http://www.bilingualamerica.com/main/careers.htm
Instructors and Sales Positions

The Chronicle of Higher Education
http://chronicle.com/search/jobs/
Coursebridge
www.coursebridge.com
Instructors

Cyber Edit
http://www.cyberedit.com/hub/jobs.shtml
Admission and Resume editors

Eduwizards
http://eduwizards.com/index.php
Tutors

EduWriters
http://eduwriters.com/index.html
Writers and Editors

eSylvan
http://www.esylvan.com/About/AboutCareers.aspx
Certified Teachers

ETS Online Scoring Network
www.ets.org
Click careers

HomeworkHelp.com
http://www.homeworkhelp.com/tutorjoinus.php
Tutors
Pay $12.00 to $36.00 per hour

Homework Tutoring
http://www.homeworktutoring.com/work_with_us.shtml
Tutors

John Hopkins University
http://www.cty.jhu.edu/ctyonline/writing/index.html

Kidspan
http://www.kidspan.com/career.htm
Teachers

Learner's Paradise
http://www.learnersparadise.com/home/cgi-bin/homePage.pl
Teachers

Limu
http://www.limu.com/pages/teach.html
Teachers and Tutors

NimbleMind.com
http://www.nimblemind.com/instructor_application_new.asp
Instructors

NRGBridge.com
http://www.nrgbridge.com/
Tutors

OnlineLearning.net
http://www.onlinelearning.net/InstructorCommunity/prospective.html?s=92
0.50600783d.1717109k40
Instructors

Pearson Educational Measurement
http://www.pearsonedmeasurement.com/careers/index.htm

Pearson Flexible Scoring
http://www.flexiblescoring-act.pearson.com/index.cfm?a=cat&cid=899
High School Essay Scoring Positions

Promise Cyber School
http://www.promise4all.com/teach/teach_signup.html
Teachers

Smartthinking.com
http://www.smarthinking.com/static/e-structors/positions/
Tutors

Student Questions.com
http://www.studentquestions.com/faq.php

Teachers Pay Teachers
http://www.teacherspayteachers.com/

Topics Education
http://www.topicseducation.com/about-us/about-us.cfm
Teachers

Universal Class
http://www.universalclass.com/teachonline/index.htm
Instructors, Teachers

University of California Berkeley
http://www.universalclass.com/teachonline/index.htm
Online Teachers and Professors

Virtual University
http://vu.org/proposal.html
Teachers and Instructors

Western Governer's University
http://www.wgu.edu/about_WGU/employment.asp#faculty
Mentors

Wyzant
http://www.wyzant.com/
Teachers, Tutors and Mentors

Engineering

Ana1og
http://www.analogone.com/Company/Jobs/jobs.html
Engineers and Bench Technicians

EBI Consulting
http://www.ebiconsulting.com/CareersPage.aspx
Engineers and Technical Support

Health Care

Fonemed
www.fonemed.com
Registered Nurses Only

IntelliCare
http://www.intellicare.com/careers/intellicare_careers.php
Registered Nurses

McKesson
http://www.mckesson.com/en_us/McKesson.com/Careers/Careers.html

MedZilla
http://www.medzilla.com/findjobs.html

SHS Careers
http://www.shsinc.com/

Human Resources & Staffing

Cyber Search Consultants
http://www.cscrecruiters.com/careers.htm
Consultants

Diedre Moire Corporation, Inc.
http://www.diedremoire.com/main.asp?uri=1060&mn=13&sti=256
Recruiters

EEG Recruiting
http://www.eegrecruiting.com/
Technical and Professional Recruiters

Enid Chesterfield & Company
http://www.enidchesterfield.com/career.php
Recruiters

ERE.net
http://jobs.ere.net/
Various

Healthcare Recruiters International
http://www.hcrintl.com/default.cfm?page=113
Recruiters

HRAdvice.com
http://www.hradvice.com/contact.html
Human Resource Professionals

IRES, Inc.
http://www.iresinc.com/careers.html#careers
Executive Recruiters, Staffing Consultants, Healthcare Recruiters,
Science/Chemistry Recruiters, and Personnel Research Assistants

Staffing Force
https://staffingforce.com/StaffingProWebSite/MakeMoney.aspx
Staffing Associate

Legal

Counsel On Call
http://www.counseloncall.com/
Attorney and Paralegal

E.P. Dine Legal Search
http://www.epdine.com/jobs.html

Law Offices of Ismail Laher
http://www.immigrationabc.com/Immigration-jobs.htm
Attorneys, Law Clerks, Legal Assistants, Immigration Issues Specialists, Filing
assistants, Web persons, Data specialists

MicroMash
www.micromashbar.com
Bar Exam Mentors

Moyer Paralegal Services
http://www.moyerparalegal.com/
Paralegals

Real Solutions, LLC
http://www.clicknclose.net/index.html

Loan Officers

Crossroad Financial Services LLC
www.crossroadfinancial.com

Nationwide Loan Processing
www.loanprocessor.org
Contract Processors

NetBranch.com
www.loanofficer.com
Loan Officers, Originators, Financial Service Agents, Realtors

NLC National Lending Corporation
www.mynlc.com
Loan Originators

Medical Transcription, Transcribers, Coders

A&W Medical Transcription Service
www.awmedtranscripiton.com/contact_us

Absolute Document Services
http://www.absolutedocs.com/careers.htm

Advanced Transcription
http://www.advancedtx.com/employment.php

AllTranscription.com
www.alltranscripiton.com/careers.html

Amphion Medical
www.amphionmedical.com

Arkees Incorporated
www.askmthouse.com/join.htm

Ascend Healthcare Systems
www.ascendhealthcare.com/employment.htm

Avaz MD,
www.avazgroupllc.com/s2/careers01.html

Aviacode Incorporated
http://www.aviacode.com/
Medical Coders

Bestscribe Transcription,
www.bestscribe.net

Brown & Meyers
www.brownmeyers.com/contact.shtml

Code Busters
www.codebusters.com
Coders

The Coding Network
http://www.aviacode.com/
Coders

Complete Coding Solutions
http://www.completecodingsolutions.com/jobs.html
Coding Consultants

Crain's Diversified Services,
www.crainsservice.com

CRS Transcription
www.freewebs.com/crstranscription.com

Datakey MT
www.datakeymt.com

Davies Transcription Service
www.davmarpad.com

The Doctor's Note
www.thedoctorsnote.net

DSG Medical Transcription Solutions
http://www.dsg-inc.net/careers.aspx

Eagle's Landing Transcription Service
www.elts.net

Effiscribe
www.effiscribe.com

Emdat,
www.emdat.com

Emtex
www.emtex.be

Express Document
www.expressdocument.net

Global Med Data
www.globalmeddata.net/new/default.asap

Management Support Services Inc
www.mssitrans.com

Medical Scribe Consultants LLC
www.medicalscribeconsultants.com

Medical Transcription
www.medicaltranscription.org

Medical Transcription Company
www.themedicaltranscriptioncompany.com

Medico Trans
www.medicotrans.com

MedRec Resources LLC
www.medrecresources.com

MedScribe
www.medscribellc.com

MxSecure Inc,
www.mxsecure.com

NetDictation
www.netdictation.com

Perfect Transcription LLC
www.perfecttranscription.com

Perfect Word Processing Inc.
www.pwp-mt.com

Preferred Physician's Transcription Inc
www.preferredtranscription.com

Professional Medical Services
www.professionalmedicalservices.org

Rapid Transcript
www.rapidtranscript.com

Serviss Transcription
www.servisstranscription.com

Sten-Tel
www.sten-tel.com

Taurus Data Links Pvt. Ltd.
www.taurusdatalinks.com

Transcend Services
www.transcendservices.com

Transcription Tree
www.transcriptiontree.com

Transmed
www.medicalscribes.com

Viva Medical Transcription Services
www.vivacorporation.com

WaveScribe
www.wavescribe.com/home.htm

WHIN On Time Transcription
www.whin.net.educational/transcription.html

Worldtech Medical Technology Services
www.worldtechusa.com

ZyDoc
www.zydoc.com

Not for Profit (Nonprofit) Opportunities

Philanthropy
www.philanthropy.com

Idealist.org
www.idealist.org

Notary

American Signing Connection
http://www.americansigningconnection.com/additional.html

CDS Signing Services
http://www.cdssigning.com/

Signing Source
http://www.signingsource.com/p_notaries.asp

Vital Signing, Inc.
http://www.vitalsigning.com/notary.html

Proofreaders

PaperCheck
http://www.papercheck.com/editors.html
Editors

Online Jurors

Ejury
www.ejury.com

Jury Test
www.jurytest.com

Jury Insights
http://www.mockjuror.com/

Online Verdict.com
www.onlineverdict.com

Trial Practices Inc
www.trialpractice.com

ZapJury.com
www.zapjury.com

Technical Job Opportunities

Alchemic Dream
http://www.alchemicdream.net/jobs.php

Allied Web
http://www.awwg.net/jobs.php

Ancient Geek
www.ancientgeek.com/careers

Arise (tech support)
www.arise.com

Art & Logic
www.artlogic.com/careers
Software Developers

Ask Dr. Tech
www.askdrtech.com

Best-Templates
http://www.best-templates.net/jobs.htm
Web Designers

ComputerAssistant.com
http://www.computerassistant.com/
 Mobile Computer Support Technicians

CorpImages.net
http://www.corpimages.net/english/EmploymentProgram.html
Freelance Web Programmers

CRMGriot.com
http://www.crmgriot.com/careers.htm
Consultants

Devi Studios
http://www.devistudios.com/jobs.htm
ScreenWriters and Technical Assistants

Digital Fusion, Inc.
http://www.fusiongames.com/work.htm
Programmers and Artists

Driver Guide
http://www.driverguide.com/hiring.htm
Database Helpers

First Beat Media
http://www.firstbeatmedia.com/jobs.html
Search Engine Optimization Specialists, Writers and Content Managers,
various technical positions

Geeks On Time
http://www.geeksontime.com/working-with-geeks.aspx
Technicians

Grindstone
http://grindstone.com/career.html

Laboratory Expertise Center
http://www.labexpertise.com/careers/positions.htm
Various Technical Jobs

LanceAdvance
http://lanceadvance.com/index.php
Various Technical Jobs

Leap Development
http://www.leapdevelopment.com/leap_jobs.php
Web Developers and Graphic Designers

Lovell Technology
http://www.lovelltechnology.com/jobs.html
Web Designers, Programmers, Hosting Support Staff and Various Other
Technical Jobs

Momentum Network
http://www.momentumnetwork.com/page.php?pg=careerop
Online Support Technicians
Graphic Designers
Database Integration Programmers
Web/Software Developers

Marketing Project Managers
Train the Trainer/Coach Specialists
Business Development Managers

Moonlight Mobile
http://www.moonlightmobile.com/joinus.htm
Programmers, Graphic Designers, Software Engineers, Content Specialists
and Web Designers

My SQL AB
http://www.mysql.com/about/jobs/index.html
Various Technical Positions

php Freelancers
http://www.php-freelancers.com/
Freelance Opportunities

PlumChoice
http://www.plumchoice.com/careers.asp
Various Professional and Technical Positions

Quality Automation
http://www.qualityautomation.com/employment_v2.asp
Various Technical and Support Positions

Rent A Coder
http://www.rentacoder.com/RentACoder/DotNet/default.aspx?
Bid on Coding Jobs

Scriptlance
http://www.scriptlance.com/
Respond to Various Posted Projects

Spider Splat
http://spidersplat.com/about_jobs.htm

Support Freaks
http://supportfreaks.com/joinourteam.html
Various Technical Opportunities

Technical Outsourcing
www.technicaloutsourcing.com
Respond to projects

TechWriters.com
http://www.techwriters.com/
Technical Writers

U-C Webs
http://www.u-cwebs.com/careers.htm
Website Optimizers and SEO Specialist

USPages
http://www.u-cwebs.com/careers.htm
Web Page Designers

Virtuo Group
http://www.virtuogroup.com/index.html
Various Technical

Telemarketing & Sales

Access Ability USA -
www.access-ability-usa.net

ASI
http://www.flutternet.com/flutternet/pages/careers.htm

Blue Zebra
www.bluezebra.com

Brighten Communications
www.brightenemployment.com

Christian Home Advertising
www.christianhomeadvertising.com

Class USA
www.class-usa.com

Discontinued Item
www.discontinueditem.com

Eagle Productions
www.eagleproductions.net

Global Safe Technologies, Inc.
www.safesolution.com

GPHoffice
www.gphoffice.com

Grindstone
www.grindstone.com

Health Services
www.healthsvc.com

Hot Point Marketing
www.hotpointmarketing.com

Intelemark
www.Intelemark.com

Intrep
www.intrep.com

Kardel Telemarketing Services
www.kardelmarketing.com

Knowledge Anywhere
www.knowledgeanywhere.com

NewTarget
www.new-target.com

OPK Telemarketing
www.opktelemarketing.com

Rich Enterprises, Inc.
http://www.richworldwide.com/careers.htm

Special Data Processing
www.specialdata.com

Synergroup Systems
www.synergroup.com

Telereachjobs
www.telereachjobs.com

The Strategic Media Group
www.thestrategicmediagroup.com

Trigger Touch
http://www.triggertouch.com/html/jobs.html

Vending Placement
www.vendingplacement.com

Virtual Tour USA
www.virtualtourusa.com

Your Town Community Guide
www.ytcg.com

Transcription

A/V Tronics
www.avtronics.com

Absolute Document Service
www.yourremoteoffice.com

Accentance
www.accentance.com

Accurate Typing
www.accuratetyping.net

Accuscribe
www.accuscribe.net

Accutran Global
www.accutranglobal.com

ADS
www.absolutedocs.com/careers.htm

Alice Darling Secretarial Services
http://alicedarling.com/

American High Tech Transcription
www.htsteno.com

Axolotl
www.axolotl.com

BTC Worldwide
www.btcworldwide.com

BVS
www.bvstranstech.com

Cambridge Transcription
www.ctran.com/employ.htm

Caption Colorado
www.captioncolorado.com

Cherry Lane Print
http://cherrylane.com/About-Us/Employment-Opportunities.aspx
Guitar Transcribers and Piano Arrangers

Chromolume Transcription
www.chromolumeinc.com/transcription/employ.html

CHS
www.chswebsite.org

CyberDictate
www.cyberdictate.com

CyberSecretaries
www.youdictate.com

Cymetirx
www.hmsintl.com

Cypher Services, Inc.
www.cyphercontractors.com

Diversified Reporting
www.diversifiedreporting.com

Domenichelli Business Services
www.moderdayscribe.com

Escribeology
carrie@escribeology.com

Escriptionist
www.escriptionsit.com

Executive Branch
www.mannartgallery.com/EB.html

Express Document Service
www.expressdocument.net/index.html

Fantastic Transcripts
www.fantastictranscripts.com
Boston Residents Only

Health Services
www.healthsvc.com

JA Media Services
www.jamedia.com

Legal Stenography
www.legaltranscription.com

Lighthouse Documents
www.lighthousedocuments.com

Mass Transcription
www.masstranscription.com

Medicaltranscription.org
www.medicaltransription.org/emloyment1.html

Medquist
www.medquist.com

Morning Side Partners
www.morningsidepartners.com

Mountain West Processing
www.mountainwestprocessing.com

MTJobs
www.mtjobs.com

Mulberry Studio
www.mulberrystudio.com/jobs.htm

NDR
www.ndr-inc.com

Neal R. Gross
www.nealrgross.com

Net Transcripts
http://www.nettranscripts.com/nt_employment.htm

Onsite3
http://www.onss.com/

OSI – Transcription
www.ositranscription.com

Perfect Transcription
http://perfecttranscription.com/careers.shtml

Production Transcripts
www.productiontranscripts.com

Purple Shark Transcriptions
http://www.purpleshark.net/pstwork.htm

Rapidtext
www.rapidtext.com

Regal Transcription Company
www.regaltrans.com

RTO Stat
www.rtostat.com

Scribes
www.scrivetrans.com/employ.html

SpeakWrite
www.speak-write.com

Spectra Medi
www.spectramedi.com

Start Script
www.startscript.com

Steno Scripts
www.stenoscripts.com

Talk 2 Type
www.talk2type.net

Task Document Services
www.usetask.com

The Back Suite Corporation
http://thebacksuite.com

The Transcription Agency
www.thetranscriptionagency.com

The Transcription Company
www.trascripts.net

Tiger Fish
www.tigerfish.com

Trans Health
www.transhealth.com

Transcend Services
www.transcendservices.com

Transcription 2000
www.transcription-services.org/support.html

Transcription Service, Inc
www.tsitranscripts.com/careers.html

Type Write Transcription
www.typewp.com

Ubiqus
www.ubiqus.com

United Tran
www.unitedtran.com

Viable Technologies
http://www.viabletechnologies.com/jobs.php

Vitac
www.vitac.com

Wordz Xpressed
www.wordzexpressed.com

World Wide Dictation
www.worldwidedictation.com

Translation

ABC Translation Services
http://www.translationsabc.com/signup.html

Academic Word
http://www.academicword.com/emp.asp

Accurapid Translations
www.accurapid.com

Aero Translations
www.aerotranslations.com

Affordable Language Translations
www.affordablelanguageservices.com

Affordable Translation Services
www.affordabletranslations.com

African Translation
http://www.africatranslation.com/Translators.html

Asist Translation Services
www.asisttranslations.com

Berlitz Language
http://careerservices.berlitz.com/current_job_vacancies.asp

Bilingual America, Inc.
http://www.bilingualamerica.com/main/careers.htm

Bridge-Linguatec
https://www.bridgelinguatec.com/

Butler Hill Group
http://www.butlerhill.com/job/index.html

Global Link
http://www.globalinktranslations.com/work_with_us.asp?section=workwithus

Ie Center
www.ie-center.com

Japan Pacific Publications
http://www.japanpacific.com/english/e_translation.html

Language Translation, Inc
http://www.languagetranslation.com/

Language Line Services
http://www.languageline.com/page/careers/

Languages Unlimited
http://www.languagesunlimited.com/index.php

Linguist List
http://linguistlist.org/jobs/index.html

Linguistic Systems
http://www.linguist.com/for-translators-overview.htm

LionBridge
http://www.lionbridge.com/lionbridge/en-US/company/work-with-us/freelance.htm

MultilingualVacancies.com
Job vacancies

National Virtual Translation Center
http://www.nvtc.gov/employment.html

Network Omni
http://www.networkomni.com/about-careers.asp

New World Language Services
http://www.newworldlanguages.com/

Open World Translations
http://www.openworldtranslations.com/jobs.htm

Pacific Interpreters
http://www.pacificinterpreters.com/

Patent Interpreters
www.patentinterpreters.com

Patent Translations, Inc.
www.patenttranslations.com

Pro Translators
www.protranslators.com

SDL International
www.sdl.com

Set Systems Translation Services
http://www.set-systems.com/eng/cu_app1_en.asp

Telelanguage.com
www.telelanguage.com

Top Line Aid
www.toplineaid.com

Trally.com
ww.trally.com

UC Translations
http://www.uctranslations.com/careers.html

We-Translation.com
www.we-translate.com

WinTranslation
http://www.wintranslation.com/employment.html

WisDeal Corporation
http://www.wisdeal.com/jobs.html

Writing Opportunities

About.com
http://freelancewrite.about.com/od/?once=true&

Academic Word
http://www.academicword.com/emp.asp

Allworth Press
http://www.allworth.com/Articles.asp?ID=124

Appingo
www.appingo.com

Associated Content
www.associatedocntent.com/join.html

Author101
www.author101.com

BackStage Jobs
http://backstagejobs.com/jobs.php

Blogitive
http://blogitive.com/

Brandon Hall
http://www.brandon-hall.com/about/about.shtml

Investigative Reporters & Editors, Inc.
www.ire.org

Edit Fast
www.editfast.com

Edu Writers
www.eduwriters.com

Freelancers Wanted
www.freelancers-wanted.com

Freelance Writing Gigs
www.freelancewritinggigs.com

Funds For Writers
www.fundsforwriters.com

My Essays
www.myessays.com

Pay Per Post
www.payperpost.com

ReviewMe
www.reviewme.com

Write For Cash
www.writeforcash.com

Writer Find
www.writerfind.com

Online Recruiters for Home Workers

Aquent
www.acquent.com

FlexibleExecutives
http://www.flexibleexecutives.com/
Various Executive Recruting opportunities

MomCorps
www.MomCorps.com

Part-TimeProfessionals
www.Part-timeProfessionals.com

Online Magazine for Work at Home Professionals
www.wahm.com
Various job listings

Sologig
www.sologig.com

WorkSpace
www.workspace.liveops.com
Social Networking site featuring job leads and resources

A B O U T THE AUTHOR

Princess Clark-Wendel, MBA is no stranger to success. As a highly regarded, respected and accomplished comprehensive planning and design specialist her credentials and stellar skill set hail from both education and experience. She is a graduate of the well renowned Booth School of Business at the University of Chicago and her experience crosses several industries. Since 1989, she has worked to strengthen people and organizations by developing solid practices and principals that has led to widespread success over various genres and industries. These strategies have opened many doors for her clients that has included; new and innovative revenue generation tactics,

acquisition of additional funding, new employment and career opportunities as well as asset protection and legacy building initiatives. These things has developed her mantra and shaped her mission of helping her clients to live the American dream - worry free!